PRAISE FOR *THE SPIRIT'S FRUIT: A PARTICIPATORY STUDY GUIDE*

I am grateful for David Moffett-Moore's latest contribution to spirituality and faith development. This down-to-earth resource is an attempt to connect faith to everyday life, using the Bible as a primary resource in that effort.

This particular study guide, *The Spirit's Fruit*, begins with an issue the author has faced in his own life: anger. It then uses the nine gifts of the Spirit to inform how each of those gifts might assist in coming to terms with that issue. One can easily make the jump from anger to some other issue and apply the lessons.

Throughout the study guide, the author mixes in quotations from multiple sources, both academic and folksy. Those, along with his own insights, help to shape an easy-to-read means toward understanding the nine gifts, and seeing how they are present in the real world. Even as each gift is explored, there is an overall theme: Letting God inspire and lead us from the inside produces a focus away from self toward others. That shift will assist us in expressing the love, joy, peace, patience, kindness, goodness, gentleness, faithfulness and self-control that we all want. The guide is not a guilt-trip book that sets us up for failure, but an encouragement toward a goal. None of us will have all nine gifts operating at the same time at the same level, but we are invited into seeing how we can take steps forward.

Rev. David Hedlin
Peace Evangelical Lutheran Church (ELCA), New Lenox, IL

We don't often take notice of it, but Paul wrote a lot about food. He writes about the Lord's Supper. He writes about how the early Christians treated each other around food. There were arguments about what was right and not right to eat. The author invites us to the table – to share, in community – and to reflect together – on the fruits of the Spirit. He sits with us as we engage the scriptures and our own stories to create a recipe for one laughing, healthy body where we are in community!

This fresh look at the fruits of the Spirit, from a pastor's heart, will be nourishment for the soul and dessert for the mind. It is easy to imagine a congregation, gathered around a table covered with good fruit, asking each other the questions that arise from this study. Christ's presence is known in sharing such a meal. Come to the table!

Rev. Michael Mather
Broadway United Methodist Church, Indianapolis, IN

I was pleasantly surprised when reviewing *The Spirit's Fruit: a Participatory Study Guide*, I expected a rehash of studies I have led or sermons preached. What I found was a basic, balanced and biblical guide to refresh my spiritual growth.

The **Biblical teaching** section was simple but not simplistic.

Call to reflection with the challenging questions caused me to evaluate my Christian obedience and the depth of my dependance on the Spirit's gifts.

Call to Conversation questions instilled a desire to seek out others and engage in a transparent discussion.

Call to Action was practical and achievable with God's help in one's daily experience.

Prayer, a fitting close to each lesson, inspired me to add my own words.

I believe this study guide will prove to be a great resource for Christian growth especially if incorporated with a sermon series followed by small group discussion.

I recommend Dave's Study Guide for students who are not afraid to encounter scripture, examine personal faith and enlist in practical service for Christ. This is an excellent resource to help a Christian "bear the fruit as he or she becomes the fruit" (page 4).

Thanks Dave for your personal sharing sprinkled throughout the lessons. Your testimony kept the material applicable (especially to one who also had a violent temper) and my anticipation for in the next lesson.

Rev. Ronald Devenport
Pastor, Mill Creek Baptist Church, 39 years

With the gracious good humor and willingness to be vulnerable that we've come to expect from him, the Rev. Dr. David Moffett-Moore encourages us to live a "fruit-filled life" with Jesus Christ – and with one another. Written for use by Sunday School classes, small groups, and individuals, *The Spirit's Fruit* fulfills beautifully the grand goal set for this series by Energion Publications: "Scholarship in service." Summary reflections, well-posed questions, and prayers mined from the treasury of church history conclude each chapter. Moffett-Moore deftly guides us as we ponder each "fruit of the Spirit" in turn, coaxing us to look at Jesus Christ, to look at ourselves, and to look at exemplars who have gone before us in faith. This is an eminently practical volume, yet one marked by solid study not only of the Letter to the Galatians but of the breadth of the Bible. Read this book – and bear the fruit of the Spirit!

The Rev. Steven M. Mullin
Honorably Retired, Presbyterian Church (U.S.A.)

THE SPIRIT'S FRUIT

A PARTICIPATORY STUDY GUIDE

DAVID MOFFETT-MOORE

Energion Publications
Gonzalez, FL
2014

Cover Design: Henry Neufeld

ISBN10: 1-938434-84-6
ISBN13: 978-1-938434-84-6
Library of Congress Control Number: 2014936507

Energion Publications
P. O. Box 841
Gonzalez, FL 32560

Web: energion.com
E-mail: pubs@energion.com
850-525-3916

Acknowledgments

Every book is always a group effort.

This book exists because the church I serve, St. Peter's United Church of Christ, granted me a sabbatical month during which I could focus on writing. It exists because St. Peter's supports my ministry with them. A rough draft became the basis for our Bible study group; each member of the group contributed to the development and improvement of this text. I owe a debt of appreciation to David and Cathy Dutro, Ralph Eisenbrandt, Carol Gilday, Marilyn McManimen, Mary Rahm and Dick Trevarthian. Two colleagues read through the manuscript, helping to point out errors and weaknesses. I thank Rev. Susan Lynch and Rev. David Alfeld-Johnson for their kind and careful insights. My wife Becki also read it and offered her perspective. All of these people contributed to the improvement of the original manuscript and to them all I am grateful. As to what improvements yet need to be made, I will accept responsibility for them. I encourage the reader to mark and highlight and comment while reading the text, to help make it your own. Simply reading the book alone will not accomplish anything; it must transfer the hope and joy I have experienced while researching and writing, so that the fruit of the Holy Spirit may truly take root and grow in your life!

Grace and Peace!

The Participatory Study Series

The Participatory Study Series from Energion Publications is designed around the motto "scholarship in service." Each guide is written by someone with a strong background in the topic studied and designed for use by lay people in Sunday School classes and small groups, as well as for individual study.

These guides are not all easy reading. Some of the topics covered require serious effort on the part of the student. But the guides do provide all the resources necessary for a fruitful study.

The section "Using this Book" is designed for the series but adapted to the particular study guide. Each author is free to emphasize different resources in the study, and to follow his or her own plan in presenting the material.

It is our prayer at Energion Publications that each study guide will lead you to a deeper understanding of your Christian faith.

– Henry Neufeld, General Editor

USING THIS BOOK

This study guide is will be found very helpful for small groups, such as Sunday School classes. Individual students working on their own will benefit from the stimulation it provides. It might serve as an introductory textbook.

The book itself will give you with an overview of a topic, The Spirit's Fruit (Galatians 5:22-25), providing specific questions for discussion. There are several things you can do to make your study more profitable.

(1) Where **resources** are suggested, divide them between members of the class and consult them during your study time. Students can bring what they have learned to the class. This is also a good time to help your church improve its library. Suggest some of these resources for your library shelves.

(2) **Share.** The Participatory Study Guides to Bible books pioneered sharing as an integral part of your study, but it will work just as well when you are studying a topic. Sharing does not mean harassing other people with your viewpoint. It's a matter of listening and being accountable in your community. If you come to a conclusion, listen to others who can comment on it and possibly point out reasons that you may be wrong, or ideas that may not have occurred to you.

This is the second topical guide in this series. It is exceptionally practical. Be sure to think of living the word as you learn it!

TABLE OF CONTENTS

I

INFORMATION: WHY THIS?

When I was a boy, I had a really wicked temper. It was short and it was brutal. I would get in fights every recess. I got "C's" in Citizenship, which for most classmates was an automatic "A." A "C" in Citizenship was like getting an "F" in any other subject. It meant I did not play well with others, I did not get along, and I had a vicious temper.

My teacher took me out into the hall when I was in fourth grade. "David, I don't know what I'm going to do with you. I've kept you in during recess. I've set you in the corner. I've sent you to the principal's office. I've sent notes home to your parents. I'm at my wit's end, and I don't know what else to do. What do I have to do to get you to behave and not to fight?"

It was a serious question and she was genuinely puzzled.

In sixth grade, a classmate came over to play and accidentally hit me with a toy. I flew off the handle and sent her home. She apologized and nearly cried, but I was insistent. She was cute as a button, one of our class cheerleaders and had a crush on me, but I did not care. Even though it was an accident, I was angry. She went home and that ended the crush.

One of my friends in high school had a set of boxing gloves. We put together a make-shift boxing ring and took turns boxing with each other. My turn came along; my partner was taller with longer arms and a greater reach. He'd also boxed some with his older brothers and his father. We put the gloves on and went at it, and I went berserk. The next thing I knew, he was cowering in a corner and the rest of the gang was busy holding me down until I cooled off.

Early in my first marriage we were playing double solitaire one night, a game that requires speed. I couldn't play fast enough and lost every game, but we kept playing. Unlike Charlie Brown playing checkers with Lucy, I knew I would win a game.

She asked, "David, why are you angry?"

"I'm not angry!" I protested.

"If you're not angry, then why are you yelling and why are you pounding the table?"

"I'm not . . ." I shouted and realized I was indeed pounding the table.

I have an anger management issue.

Over the years, I've tried a number of different techniques. Most of them did not work. I can count to ten, but that just gives me time to build up a good head of steam. Taking long, slow, deep breaths requires me to be aware of the rising anger before it peaks. Walking away from the situation requires a lot of self-control and runs counter to my fighting instincts.

Philosophically, I am a pacifist. I agree that violence is never a solution, that we can reason things out together. Emotionally, I'm a fighter, and too often, my emotions win out. I realize that anger can have a good side; anger can give us energy and determination to do a task that needs to be done. I also realize anger has a significant down side as well.

There may be psychological or emotional wounds as a result of anger that go far deeper and last far longer than any physical wounds. Losing one's temper may reflect a lack of self-confidence as well as a lack of self-control. Frustration and depression can be forms of self-directed anger.

In my Bible study and as part of my personal discipline, I memorize verses of scripture. I do not remember the instance, but I stumbled across Galatians 5:22-23: "The fruit of the Spirit are these: first of all love, then joy, then peace, patience, kindness, goodness, gentleness, faithfulness and self-control. Against these, there is no Law." There are only nine, not ten, but it is a good list. Love, joy, peace, patience, kindness, goodness, gentleness, faithfulness, self-control. Reciting these has helped me immensely with my anger management issue, especially when the list ends with self-control. It is hard to fly off the handle when I start with love and joy and end with self-control. They remind me that our life together in the faith as Christians is called to be a fruit-filled life.

Having a ready supply of scripture verses stored in our memory can be a helpful resource for our daily lives. Most of us learned to memorize certain passages in Sunday School, Vacation Bible School or Confirmation classes. We've learned the Lord's Prayer, the Twenty-Third Psalm, maybe the Ten Commandments and perhaps a few others. Knowing more is better than knowing less. In Jesus' temptation with the Devil, we are reminded that even Satan can quote scripture! Knowing a variety of passages that can apply to different situations can be a help in our daily lives, just as affirmations or breath prayers can help us find and focus on the way we would go.

As Christians, our lives are gifted. We are gifted with the Holy Spirit, gifted with the spirit of Christ. Paul writes in Romans 12:6-8 and 1 Corinthians 12:8-12 about the gifts of the Holy Spirit and reminds us that we each have some of the gifts: gifts of healing, teaching, helping, serving, speaking, interpreting, and giving. "There is a variety of gifts, but one Spirit who gives them" (1 Cor 12:4). We all are gifted; we have all received the gift of the Holy Spirit. We each get some of the gifts; none of us get all of the gifts.

The fruit of the Spirit is different. Jesus tells us in John 15:1-6 that we are all to bear much fruit, and our fruit is to excel in quality and in quantity. Jesus tells us the way we are to bear fruit is by abiding in him, as a branch bears fruit by abiding in the vine. Paul gives us a list of spiritual fruit in Galatians 5:22-23. While we each get some of the gifts of the Spirit, everyone gets all of the fruit of the Spirit. We are all called to bear the fruit of love, joy, peace, patience, kindness, goodness, gentleness, faithfulness and self-control. We all bear all the fruit! This is the essence of living a fruit-filled life. We are all fruitful; we all bear all the fruit, each in its season.

When Paul describes the gifts of the Holy Spirit in Romans 12 and 1 Corinthians 12, he always speaks in the plural, "gifts." In Galatians 5:22-23, when Paul speaks of the fruit of the Holy Spirit, he speaks in the singular. There are a variety of gifts of the Spirit, but only one fruit. The fruit may be variously described and experienced, yet it remains a singular fruit. The various characteristics of this one fruitful Spirit are listed and will be considered, but in this consideration we need to keep in mind that the fruit is one, the fruitful life is one, as we are all one in the Spirit.

The fruit also fall into three categories, based upon our relationships: those that relate to God (love, joy, peace), those that relate to others (patience, kindness, goodness, faithfulness) and those that relate to us personally (gentleness, self-control.) The fruitful life is a life integrating ourselves with God and with others. Just as God consists of a Trinity, however we choose to describe it: Father-Son-Holy Spirit; Creator-Redeemer-Sustainer; The One who Forms us, Frees us, and Fills us; the Source of all Being, the Eternal Word, the Life-giving Spirit, so we are in a trinity in our relationships: God, others, self. The fruit of the Spirit are all inter-related and may overlap, with nuances in their meaning. The fruitful life depends upon harmony and balance in these relationships. The fruit of the Spirit is not just something we bear, as a tree or a vine bears fruit, it is something we are; as we bear the fruit, we become the fruit. This is the essence of a fruitful life: bearing the fruit to become the fruit.

We all have issues. The hard truth is that we are all works in progress, as Paul writes, "No one is perfect, no not one... All have sinned and fallen short of the glory of God."(Rom 3:10, 23) As Hebrews says, we have a "sin that sticks closely to us" (Heb 12:1). Your issue may not be anger; maybe it is sarcasm or selfishness. Jesus tells a parable (Matt 12:43-45 and Luke 11:24-26) of an evil spirit cast out, wandering around, and returning again with seven other evil spirits because its place was left empty. Focusing on the fruit of the Spirit can be a way for us not only to cast off the evil we don't want to do, but also to fill our spirit with the goodness of

God so the evil cannot return. Focus on the positive helps eliminate the negative!

A Call to Reflection

Recall a time when someone was angry with you. How did you feel? How did you respond to their anger?

What is your "issue"? What personality fault or character flaw most vexes you?

How can focusing on the positive can help eliminate the negative?

A Call to Conversation

When was the last time you were really angry? What provoked you then? What were the consequences? How did you recover?

What was your childhood like? Do you remember getting into fights or arguments? What usually provoked you? How did you outgrow them?

What are some of your favorite scripture passages? How have they helped you in your daily situations?

A Call to Action

Take a fifteen to twenty minute walk. While walking, take long slow deep breaths. Breathing in to slowly fill your lungs. Hold that breath. Then exhale slowly and completely. Feel both the fullness and the emptiness of each breath. While walking and breathing, recite to yourself these nine fruit of the Holy Spirit: love, joy, peace, patience, kindness, goodness, gentleness, faithfulness, self-control. Ask yourself if this physical and spiritual exercise of walking, breathing and reciting, has had any affect on your body: Are you more relaxed? Has your heartbeat slowed? Might this devotional exercise be a good way to take a break during your day?

A Call to Prayer

My dearest Lord, be thou a bright flame before me, be thou a guiding star above me, be thou a smooth path beneath me, be thou a kindly shepherd behind me, this day and for ever more. Amen. — St. Columba

2

LOVE

ove is the first and greatest commandment, the second commandment that makes it relatable, and the new commandment. Paul lists love as the greatest gift of the Holy Spirit, the first fruit of the Holy Spirit, the fulfillment of the Law and a debt we can't repay. John tells us that God is love and that the love of God is made complete in our love for one another (1 John 4:7-12). Love is a big deal!

When Jesus is asked by a lawyer, one who has studied the Jewish law of the Old Testament, what is the first and greatest commandment, Jesus replies with the *Shema* of Israel, the verse that every Jew offered every morning and every evening, every time they left their home and every time they returned. "Hear, O Israel: the Lord, the Lord our God, is One. You shall love the lord your God with all your heart and all your mind and all your strength and all your soul" (Deut 6:4-5).

The verse in Deuteronomy calls us to love God with all our heart and soul and strength; it does not include loving God with all our mind. When I study the teachings of Jesus, I know that much of what he says is found in the Old Testament. Jesus was Jewish and a rabbi, so of course the Old Testament formed his own faith. When Jesus is quoting a passage from what we call the Old Testament and what was for him the only scripture he knew, I find it interesting to see what he changes. In this passage, he adds the love of God with all our mind. Christianity is called by our founder to be an intelligent faith; we are to love the Lord our God with all our mind. A classic of the Greek mystical tradition is entitled *The Pursuit of Divine Wisdom*. St. Anselm described this intellectual love of God as "faith seeking understanding." The point is to love God with all we've got, including our minds.

Then Jesus continues, "The second is like unto the first;" it is similar and related to the first, it describes it in another way, it makes it personal and tangible. "Love your neighbor as you love yourself" (Lev 19:18). Another passage from the Old Testament. This is the entire gospel in a sentence: love God, love neighbor, love self; offering a trinity of love. The end. As Jesus says, "On these two hang all the Law and the Prophets" (Matt 22:39-41).

Not quite. The lawyer, to justify his asking the question in the first place, interrupts, "But who is my neighbor?" Jesus tells the parable of the Good Samaritan. "Who was the neighbor?" Jesus then asks. Not the priest, not the Levite, not the scribe, all of whom walked on the other side lest they be made unclean by coming too near the one beaten and robbed along side the road. "The one who offered help to a stranger." The neighbor is not defined by proximity or geography or compatibility or similarity that is ethnic, racial, linguistic, religious, political or gender based, but based simply and exclusively on need. Helping anyone in need is equivalent with loving the God who presides over the universe, the God who is in all times and all places. Helping others is tantamount to divine worship or mystical experience. Want to know where God is found? In the lowest and the least.

There is a story of a student asking his rabbi, "Why do so few find God?" The rabbi answered, "Because few are willing to look low enough."

Gathering with his disciples in the Upper Room on the last night of his earthly existence, before he is given up, Jesus offers a farewell address in the gospel of John. He says, "A new command-ment I give to you, that you love one another, that the world may know you are my disciples. Even as I have loved you, so you love one another. Greater love than this has no one: to lay down one's life for one's friends" (John 13:34-35).

"Love one another." This is not a verse found elsewhere in the Jewish scriptures; it is one of his own design. And Jesus offers us an example; he gives himself as a role model for the kind of love he is talking about. "Love one another as I have loved you." He hasn't died for them yet, that is yet to follow, but he has already loved them. He tells us why this is so important, "that the world may know you are my disciples." How do we prove our faith? Not in reciting creeds or memorizing doctrine. And not by going to church; going to church doesn't make us a Christian any more than going to McDonalds makes us a hamburger or sitting in the garage makes us a car. Not by giving a tithe of all we possess; that was the Pharisee's claim, and he went away impenitent. Not by following all 613 rules and regulations of the Old Testament or even keeping the Ten Commandments. We can keep all ten of the Commandments and still be a louse and a jerk, but not if we love one another. That is why loving one another is what Christ calls for if we are to prove that we are his disciples. Love even to the point of laying down our lives for another.

Through most of my life I have had few people I would dare call "friends." I used to boast about numbering my friends with the fingers on one hand. I did not have very many friends, nor did I want them. Once I was asked why this was so, by someone I had grown to consider a friend. I explained, "A friend is someone who, when they call, you answer, and when they ask, you do. If they ask at midnight for you to come and get them, you go. A friend is someone for whom you are willing to die. Frankly, I don't want that obligation with too many people. It's too risky!"

She paused to choose her words. "Yes," she agreed. My definition was certainly admirable and worthy, but she might consider a different phrasing of the same thought, "A friend is someone who makes your life worth living."

I was caught short. I hadn't seen that one coming. It was the same thought, just worded differently, put positively instead of negatively; an affirmation of life rather than a threat of death. I want that kind of friend; I want friends who make my life worth living. I want to be that kind of friend for others.

Christ calls us friends and lays his life down for us.

I toy with a thought. It's Sunday morning and we gather for worship. We have a mixed congregation: "diversity without division, unity without uniformity." We say, "No matter who you are or where you are in your personal journey, you are welcome here." Without regard for race, gender, ethnicity, language, politics, preference, fashion or style. Someone with nose rings and tattoos sits next to one of our curmudgeons, who scoots over to give them space in his pew. When we get to passing the Peace in our service, he leans over to this weird stranger and whispers, "I don't know you, I don't understand you, I don't much like you. But in the name of Jesus Christ, I am prepared to die for you!" I dream of a church where that can be said and heard with authenticity and integrity, where we can dare to lay down our lives for one another and for those we do not know or understand, or even like much.

Jesus even tells us to love our enemies. We all have enemies, and I don't mean the kind that live half a world away and we never see. I mean the ones who live next door or work at our side or sleep beside us in bed. The enemies that are part of our daily lives. Jesus says we are to love them as much as we love ourselves and to be willing to lay down our lives for them.

And I want to get angry with them? Who do I think I am?

I remember a quote from the youth group: "I asked Jesus how much he loved me. He said, 'This much.' And he stretched out his arms and he died."

When he rose, he appeared to Peter, who had three times denied even knowing him, even to the point of cursing. In the most formal language he spoke anywhere, Jesus asked him, "Simon, son of John, do you love me?

"Yes, Lord, you know I love you."

"Feed my lambs." Then again, "Simon, son of John, do you love me?"

"Yes, Lord, you know I love you."

"Tend my flock." Then yet again, "Simon, son of John, do you love me?"

Peter was distressed that he asked a third time. "Yes, Lord, you know everything. You know I love you."

"Care for my little ones" (John 21:15-17).

It is a powerful scene: a three-fold affirmation to wipe out the three-fold denial. In the Greek, there is more. In his book *The Four Loves*, C.S. Lewis explains that the Greeks had different words to describe different types of love: *eros, storge, philia, agape*. Eros is, of course, erotic or romantic love. Nothing wrong with that, we're just not talking about it. *Storge* is affection, fondness, compatibility, as between co-workers or team mates. *Philia* is the love between friends and family, it typically describes our human love. *Agape*, sometimes translated charity, is sacrificial love, self-giving love, love that is unconditional. The kind of love God has for us.

In the first question, Jesus asks, "Do you *agape* me more than these others?" Do you love me unconditionally over everything else? Peter responded, "I love you as a friend." So Jesus asked a second time, "Do you love me unconditionally?" and again Peter replied, "You know I love you as a friend." The third time Jesus asked, "Do you even love me as a friend?" And Peter's heart was broken. He had denied even knowing Jesus three times. In the Upper Room, Peter had protested that he would never abandon Jesus, even if he had to die with him. When the time came, Peter cursed instead of confessed. "You know everything. You know I am weak and impulsive; I am a bragging coward. You know everything. You know, such as I am, I love you with what I have." We all have limits, faults, inconsistencies. Can we love God even with our weaknesses? Jesus promises that this love fulfills the Law and the prophets.

C.S. Lewis describes what he calls need-love and gift-love. Need-love is the love that we feel; we need to be loved as truly as we need air to breathe. Gift-love is the love that is God; it is freely given without expectation or condition and unmotivated by anything we do or don't do, God loves us no matter what.

When my son Jason was in second grade he had a writing assignment. They were all to write about the necessities of life. As with everyone else, Jason wrote about the three necessities of life,

usually described as food, shelter and clothing. Jason described
them differently. He kept food and shelter, but argued that we can
live without clothing. If it is cold or wet, we use clothing actually
as portable shelter. For Jason, the third necessity of life was love.
His teacher and I both agreed he had a good case. As much as food,
shelter or clothing, we need to love and to be loved.

In his most carefully worded letter to the Romans, Paul writes
about a Christian's duties and obligations. He concludes saying,
"Owe no one anything but to love one another, for whoever loves
their neighbor has fulfilled the law.... Love does no wrong to a
neighbor; therefore, love is the fulfillment of the Law" (Rom 13:8,
10). The Law Paul speaks of is the Jewish Law of the Old Testament. Love fulfills the Law. Love finishes the Law. There can be no
law against love.

In 1 Corinthians 12, Paul describes different gifts of the Holy
Spirit and how these gifts work together for the common good. He
reminds us that we are all gifted and we each have gifts, given by
the Spirit. Then he says, "Let me show you a more excellent way."
and begins his famous "Love Chapter," 1 Corinthians 13. He waxes
eloquently on the greatness of this love and describes its various
attributes, and then concludes, "Faith, hope and love abide, these
three, and the greatest of them all is love." Put love first. Of all the
gifts of the Holy Spirit: healing, teaching, preaching, giving, pray-
ing, discerning, helping, serving, etc., the greatest is love.

In the passage upon which this book is based, Galatians 5:22-
23, Paul lists the fruit of the Spirit. Again, love is listed as the first
fruit.

In John's ode to love, 1 John 4:7-12, he tells us that God is
love. Those who do not love do not know God, and whoever does
love does know God. As we love one another, God abides in us and
God's love is perfected in us. The Greek word here is another word
full of meaning. It is what Jesus says from the cross, "It is finished."
It is what the Spirit says in Revelation 21, "It is fulfilled." In our
love for one another, God's love is finished, fulfilled, perfected,

completed. Conversely, if we don't love one another, God's own love remains unfinished and unfulfilled.

Love, the first fruit of the Holy Spirit, the greatest gift of the Holy Spirit. Love that is of God and is God. Love that is the first and greatest commandment and the second commandment like the first and the new commandment. Loving God with all our heart and soul and mind and strength; loving our neighbor as we love ourselves, loving one another as Christ has loved us, even loving our enemies. This love fulfills the Law.

This love ought to be enough to keep me from flying off the handle, but God has provided eight more checks, just in case. Sometimes it is good to build a little redundancy into the system. Sometimes the hardest person in the world to love is one's self.

A Call to Reflection

Who is the greatest challenge for you to love? What can you do to help make that love complete?

A Call to Conversation

Remember your first infatuation. Does God love us with that passion and fire? How is saying that God is in love with us sound different from saying that God loves us?

Remember a time you felt most loved. What was that like? What led up to it? Who was involved? What were the consequences?

How does Hollywood depict love in movies and on television? How does that differ from God's description of holy love?

Jesus tells us we are to love even our enemies. How can we accomplish this? Who is someone you might regard as an enemy? How can you act with love toward them?

A Call to Action

Tell someone today that you love them: spouse, parent, child, friend. Say the words and make sure they know you mean it.

A Call to Prayer

Grant me, dearest Lord, to know you, to love you and to rejoice in you. And, if I cannot do this perfectly in this life, let me at least grow day by day until I can do them completely. Let my knowledge of you increase, let my love of you grow, let my joy in you be great, that my life may be full of your presence. You are the true God, and God of all truth; so make good your gracious promises to me, that my joy may be full and my love complete. Amen.

— From St. Augustine

3

Joy

Joy is not the first emotion that comes to mind when I am getting angry. Joy may be its exact opposite. Anger is very self-centered and self-serving. Anger is aggressive, dark and violent. The word JOY serves as an acronym: Jesus, Others, Yourself. Anger is self-centered. Joy is not. If I think of Jesus first in every situation, and then the perspective of the other people involved, and only afterward consider my own concerns, I would probably never be angry. Probably.

The joy that is spoken of here is not the joy of the drunk, carousing at night and waking with a hangover, or the joy of the champion, exulting himself as victor in a contest. This is joy that has a deep and lasting quality to it. Joy comes as a gift from outside one's self and not as a consequence of one's own efforts and endeavors. The Greek words for joy and for grace share a common root, which is an unconquerable gladness and a contagious joy.

There is a sense in which joy comes to us as a gift when we are seeking something else. There is also a sense in which lasting joy comes from deep inside of us. This is one of the paradoxes of faith: both can be true. Joy comes as gift when we give ourselves for others and joy wells up from within us.

Our transitory happiness is like a bubbling brook, full of action and noise but lacking any depth; it is easy to run dry. Joy is like the flow of a mighty river. The surface may appear calm, but underneath is a mighty current that pulls us on and a depth that will not run dry during any passing drought. This is joy that is permanent and all-pervasive, like a deep well that taps into a hidden aquifer and will not run dry through any drought on the surface.

Happiness can be based on happenstance and come from our circumstances. We can feel happy on a sunny day and lose that happiness on a cloudy one. There is a reason Seasonal Affective Disorder spells sad! Joy comes from within and does not fluctuate with the weather or change with the seasons. Happiness may be what the world gives us; joy is what we bring into the world.

Philippians 4:4 tells us, "Rejoice in the Lord always and again I say: rejoice!" We don't often see exclamation marks in scripture. The punctuation and grammar are all part of the translation, not the original Greek, and this is a good place for exclaiming, "Rejoice! Rejoice!" To rejoice is to leap, to dance, to celebrate.

Joy is elusive, like trying to catch a butterfly or chase a puppy. Better to focus on something else and let the joy find you! I discovered years ago that I cannot enjoy anything I seek to control. The mere desire to control, whether I attain it or not, eliminates any possibility of finding joy in that event. If I want to find joy, I must first abandon any attempt to control the situation. Maybe that's part of what is meant by "Let go and let God." Our willingness to trust God in a certain situation may contribute to our ability to find joy.

I've never been much of a dancer. When I was in school, the boys lined the walls and watched the girls dance with each other. Not much fun. Once, I became an exception. At a school dance, Tonya asked me to dance and before I knew to say "No," she had me on the dance floor. She could tell how uncomfortable I was, even a blind man could. "Just listen to the beat and move to the music." The DJ was playing "Jumping Jack Flash" by the Rolling Stones. It has a definite driving beat even I could follow. Soon I was moving to the music, listening to the beat and almost dancing. I think I may have thrown in some calisthenics; after all, Jack was jumping. It was exhilarating. I lost my self-consciousness and didn't worry about what others might have thought of my peculiar moves. I just danced and leapt and rejoiced with great gladness. It was ecstatic.

The word "ecstasy" comes from the Greek, meaning to be outside of one's self, beyond one's self, an experience of transcendence. Ecstasy was a religious experience, a spiritual high, of being taken outside one's self and one's consciousness and being caught up in the fullness of the moment. A holy joy. True joy is in the divine now.

Hebrews 12:2 tells us "for the joy that was set before him, Jesus endured the cross, despising its shame." I have heard, seen, read and described images of the crucifixion; the most painful way for any human to die, absolute anguish and suffering. How do you despise that? How do you count that as nothing? How great must the joy be to endure, despise and ignore such an ignoble execution! What suffering would I ever be asked to endure that would approach it? How dare I then, in my conceit, become angry about anything!

This calls for a sense of contentment with what we have, an attitude of gratitude. Socrates once said that true wealth is not in having more but in wanting less. As Paul says in Philippians 4:11, "I have learned to be content in all circumstances."

For a time I belonged to a group called Joyful Christians that published a bi-monthly newsletter and several books of jokes, anecdotes, cartoon, humorous stories, epigrams, etc. (www.JoyfulNoiseletter.com) They even had a picture available for purchase of Jesus laughing. I think he must have laughed. We know he ate, drank, slept, walked, talked, healed, grew tired, even was angry himself at those money changers in the temple. He was human in every way, as we are, "yet without sin." So he must have laughed! Though he suffered at the end, he rejoiced in between.

Joy is essentially a spiritual experience. In Romans 14:17, Paul writes, "The Kingdom of God is not eating or drinking, but righteousness, peace and joy in the Holy Spirit." He has been talking about what Christians can eat and ought not to eat, what days we ought and ought not to celebrate, etc. He wants to make the point that the Kingdom of God is about the spirit, not the flesh. Jesus talks a great deal about the Kingdom of God and describes it as a way of life here and now, not some "pie in the sky, by and by" kind of ethereal life in the clouds. His favorite example for what the Kingdom of God is like, is a wedding feast.

This puzzled me when I was young. I grew up in central Indiana, where weddings and wedding receptions took place in churches. Everyone went to the wedding, some stayed for the reception. The reception was in the fellowship hall, usually the basement. The refreshments consisted of dry cake seemingly made out of Styrofoam, topped with icing like cement with sugar in it. We had what I call "pond scum punch," punch with melted sherbet that created a foam on top. If we were lucky, we had mints and nuts. The highlight of the evening was watching the bride and the groom open their presents. If this is what heaven is like, I want some options!

My first church was in St. Joseph County, Indiana, where Notre Dame University is and two thirds of the population is Roman Catholic. My predecessor said he was doing me a favor by booking eight weddings in nine weeks, "You'll get to know the people and the community." Thanks a lot.

The location of the first reception should have been a clue: it was in the local American Legion Hall and I quickly found out why. No alcohol in the church fellowship hall, but an open bar in the Legion Hall. Fifty feet of food, every kind of meat imaginable and more ways of fixing potatoes than I had ever seen. A live band and dancing until dawn. Now I know what Jesus was talking about!

In his day, a wedding reception included the entire town and lasted for a week. One big party! The Kingdom of Heaven is like a giant wedding reception, where everybody is invited, where the food and drink is inexhaustible – this in a subsistent society, and Jesus would make it so even if he had to turn water into wine. The band plays on and we are going to celebrate, laugh and dance! Rejoice in this Lord always and again I say: rejoice! This Jesus and these others mean for you to have joy and for that joy to be full.

A Call to Reflection

When was a time you were surprised by joy, focused on something or someone else and found joy almost as a by-product?

A Call to Conversation

What are your thoughts on the tension between seeking joy and desiring control?

On anger as self-centered and joy as other-centered?

Can you describe the difference between happiness and joy in your life?

When did you bring joy to an otherwise sad situation?

Would you describe joy more as a gift from life with others or as a well-spring from within?

A Call to Action

If you could bring joy to one person, who would it be? How would you do it? Now go do it!

A Call to Prayer

Blessed are you, O Lord our God, who has nourished me from birth and who sustains all you have created. Fill our hearts with joy and gladness, that we, always having all we need in you, may rejoice to do every good work in Christ Jesus our Lord, through whom to you be glory, honor, majesty and dominion, forever and ever. Amen.

— From the Clementine Liturgy

4

PEACE

We think of peace as being more an absence than a presence. Peace is quiet and calm, as in when Jesus calmed the storm, saying, "Peace! Be still!" We think of peace as being the absence of war, which, if considered on a global scale, would be a rarity in our history. When has there been a time that we weren't fighting with one another somewhere? When the burner under my anger gets turned on, "peace" is not on my mind.

For the Greeks and Romans, certainly peace meant the absence of both organized warfare and disorganized violence. But the peace that Paul has in mind is not determined by who has the biggest stick, and it is not a peace that is established by might but by right. Tranquility and serenity are fine, but not if it comes by being beaten senselessly or unjustly. Law and order are necessary for peace, but not sufficient.

In Jeremiah 8:11, we are warned against those who say "Peace, peace" when there is no peace. We've all seen billboards and bumper stickers that say "No Christ, no peace; know Christ, know peace."

Peace and Joy, Joy and Peace, go together frequently in scripture. For early Christians, Peace and Joy were commonly used as given names: "Chara" and "Eirene." I had a fellow pastor whose wife was named Faith and whose daughters were Hope and Charity. I don't know what name he would have used if he'd had a son!

From earliest times, our towns and villages have had some official designated as the Keeper of the Peace, by whatever title, and disturbing the peace has been at least a petty crime. But I think it is interesting to note that, in his Beatitudes, Jesus did not say "Blessed are the Peacekeepers," but "Blessed are the Peace makers, for they will be called the children of God." Making peace is what Jesus is about, not keeping peace. Keeping peace might be about controlling others, but making peace is about empowering ourselves. Making peace begins with accepting ourselves as we are, honestly recognizing our strengths and our weaknesses, and to be willing to say with Popeye, "I am what I am." If we can't accept ourselves, we will never be able to accept others. Making peace can be costly as well as transformative. Making peace is work. "Burying the hatchet" can be just a way for past angers to sabotage future endeavors; better to deal with it up front and on the table, honestly and directly.

Jesus died on a cross, executed as a criminal, after leading a riot in the temple, with the charge of insurrection and rebellion over his head, "Jesus of Nazareth, King of the Jews." He did not die trying to keep peace in Jerusalem or with Rome, but making peace between heaven and earth. Making peace, not keeping peace. Our nation's military had a missile it called "the Peace-maker." I don't think that is what Jesus had in mind.

The peace Jesus had in mind was more than the absence of war or even the absence of maliciousness between neighbors or enmity in our communities. The Hebrew word for peace is *shalom*, but it means more than simple serenity or calm tranquility. Shalom means not the absence of war or violence, but the presence of all that is necessary for us to face the day calmly and confidently: peace, plenty and prosperity; health, wealth and harmony, welfare and well-being, equanimity and equality. It means everything that makes for the highest and best good, individually and collectively. It means realizing that we are all children of a loving God who wants to supply all our needs. It is more "both-and" rather than "either-or."

This is peace within each of us, peace between each of us, peace among us and peace around us, peace for communities, states, nations and worlds, peace for all God's children and all God's creation. *Shalom* in its fullness would be nothing short of heaven on earth, the Kingdom of God. A life of *shalom* is what Jesus described in his parable of the Last Judgment (Matthew 25:31-46), where everyone cares about everyone else and no one's needs go unmet.

Jesus did not die to make peace between Jerusalem and Rome, nor to free the Jewish people, nor to cleanse the temple or right the current wrongs. His death was part of bringing that Kingdom of God, the *shalom*, the peace only heaven can give.

One of the titles by which we honor Christ is "Prince of Peace." In his farewell address in John, Jesus says, "Peace I leave with you, my peace I give to you; not as the world gives, but peace that the world cannot take away... In this world you will have trouble, but peace, be of good cheer, for I have overcome the world" (John 14:27, 16:33).

Biblical peace, Christian peace, means to want the best for the other, to value the other's needs and concerns equal to our own, and to want the other's best and highest good. It is peace that is ours unconditionally, regardless of the circumstances. This peace is not dependent upon our outer circumstances but our inner confidence in our relationship with Christ, who has overcome the world and all its troubles, even our own. Peace that is confident!

My youth group designed some long sleeve T-shirts. They had the word "confidence" spelled down one sleeve. On the front was the image of a youth with a cross, standing over a lion whose eyes were crossed out. The slogan read, "I'm a confident Christian, bring on the lions!" As confident Christians, we have a peace that literally is out of this world.

When I went through my Reiki training to become a Reiki Master-Teacher, at the end of our sessions we used a Hindi word. Reiki originated in Japan and Hindi is a language from India, so it is a little incongruous. The word we ended our sessions with was *Namaste*. *Namaste* can be variously translated; it can simply mean "greetings," as in hello or good-bye. However, it is usually taken to have a much richer, fuller meaning. The best that is in me, my own truest and most complete self, greets the best that is in you, your own truest and most complete self, and wishes you peace, wellness, wholeness, completeness. The very best of me greets the very best of you and wishes you only the very best!

All the world's faith and wisdom traditions include the call to love one another, to do with others as we want done with us, to have compassion on one another.

I take it to be analogous to a Shaker greeting I've learned and used: "The Christ in me greets the Christ in thee and draws us together in love." We've used this in our worship services for Passing the Peace or Greeting One Another. We each have Christ within us. When I can get in touch with the Christ within me and open my eyes to see the Christ that is in you, then we can truly be united in Christian love, whatever we may think of our differences.

If I have this peace or want this peace, I can scarcely respond in anger, regardless of the provocation. *Peace, Shalom, Namaste*!

A Call to Reflection

Accepting ourselves is an important part of being at peace with ourselves. What do you find most difficult to accept in yourself?

Frequently, what we dislike most in others is also what we dislike in ourselves. What traits in others do you most dislike?

To what extent are they your own?

A Call to Conversation

What synonyms would you choose to describe peace?

Is there a difference between national peace and heavenly peace, between what we mean by peace and what God means?

Can you describe the difference between peace making and peace keeping? Recall a situation when you became a peace maker.

Shalom, the Hebrew word for peace, is more of a presence and an abundance than it is merely the absence of conflict. To what extent is it human effort and to what extent is it divine gift? How can we make peace more of a presence in our lives?

What are some examples of making peace in our daily lives?

A Call to Action

Who is someone that you need to make peace with? What is at issue between you? How can you begin the peace-making process? Now do it!

A Call to Prayer

Mercifully receive us, O Lord, that our adversities may be relieved and our errors amended, that we may serve you in the freedom of perfect peace. Preserve our nation's welfare in your justice and our domestic tranquility by your grace, that we may exercise all faithful devotion and witness and we may have peace in our time, through Jesus Christ our Lord. Amen.

— From the Leonine Sacramentary

5
PATIENCE

I've been told that I am not a very patient person. I contend that I have an abundance of patience; I just keep it in little tiny bottles. By "patience" we typically mean calmly waiting, enduring, resigning ourselves to a problem or condition. I suppose patience is a virtue simply because it is so rare. Patience need not exclude assertiveness, standing up for one's personal justice.

When Jason, my eldest, was a newborn, I went along to the pediatrician for his check-up. We waited over two hours in the waiting room, which is how it got its name, I suppose. When we finally got to see the doctor, I complained that I had to take off work for this visit and it was costing me money as well as time; my time was worth as much as his time. He was a little nonplussed. When we received his bill, I included a bill for my time. His office called and tried to explain that they did not pay me for my time, I only paid for his time. Again, I argued that my time was worth as much as his time and, if he expected me to wait two hours to see him, he should rightly expect to pay for that time. They did not pay me, but I never again had to wait in the waiting room!

I understand patience as a passive moment: sitting around and waiting for something to happen. I confess that I do not sit and wait well. I prefer perseverance. Patience is sitting around waiting for something to happen; perseverance is getting up and doing something to make it happen! I am better at perseverance than I am at patience.

The Greek word translated as patience has also been translated by various other terms: patience, endurance, long-suffering, forbearance, good-temper. That last one ought to rule out any burst of anger. Good temper ought to rule out any bad temper. "Patience" is a popular translation, but our modern understanding of patience lacks the depth and determination of Biblical patience. I certainly don't care for "long-suffering!" I don't even want short suffering. I prefer tenacity or equanimity.

First Maccabees says that by this "patience," Rome became master of the world. It is a conquering kind of patience, a patience that lays siege. A patience that does not make peace even in defeat, a patience that has grit and determination. A peace that Winston Churchill described when he said, "Never, never, never, never, never quit!" A patience that sets its feet, squares its shoulders and locks its jaw and with steel-eyed determination simply hangs on and wears the opposition out. This is not the way most of us would describe patience!

Ernest Hemingway describes courage as "grace under pressure." That seems a good way to describe godly patience as well. We've all been under pressure. There is no reason we can't be gracious as well.

There is a movie about the efforts and persecution of the suffragettes during the Wilson presidency entitled "Iron Jawed Angels." It is well worth seeing. If you want to see what this patience looks like, watch the women protesting for the vote in front of the White House during World War One, or locked in prison for that protest and going on a hunger strike. It is a patience that will not injure another, but neither will it bear an injury, a patience with guts and a backbone.

This is the patience that Martin Luther King, Jr. described in his sermon written in the Montgomery, Alabama jail and delivered on Christmas, 1957.

> To our most bitter opponents we say: we shall match your capacity to inflict suffering by our capacity to endure suffering. We shall meet your physical force with soul force. Do to us what you will, and we shall continue to love you. We cannot in all good conscience obey your unjust laws, because noncooperation with evil is as much a moral obligation as is cooperation with good. Throw us in jail, and we shall still love

you. Bomb our homes and threaten our children, and we shall still love you. Send your hooded perpetrators of violence into our communities at the midnight hour and beat us and leave us half dead, and we shall still love you. But be ye assured that we will wear you down by our capacity to suffer. One day we shall win freedom, but not only for ourselves. We shall so appeal to your heart and conscience that we shall win you in the process, and our victory will be a double victory.

This is patience with fire in the belly! This is the patience by which Gandhi won independence for India without any violence toward their British occupiers. The great social reform movements all exhibited a strong willed patience: anti-slavery, civil rights, suffrage, etc. I wonder if we have the intestinal fortitude for this kind of patience in our day.

John Chrysostom, a great preacher of the 4th century church (his name means "silver tongue") describes patience as a person who could avenge, but does not; someone who has both the might and the right for vengeance, but chooses not to exert it. This describes God's attitude to us. God has both the might and the right to avenge, but God chooses restraint instead. God bears with us and does not cast us off. We are to model the loving, forgiving, enduring, forbearing kind of patience we see in God and in Christ Jesus, even in the face of insult and injustice.

The ancient Stoic philosophers would respond to any situation, good or bad, with the phrase "this too shall pass," expressing a peace gained by detachment from one's circumstances. Julian of Norwich, a woman living alone while England was wracked by plague and civil war, homeless and destitute and sick with fever, repeated "all will be well and all will be well and all manner of things will be well," adding a sense of optimism in the future to the stoic's detachment in the present.

A Call to Reflection

Close your eyes and remember how it feels to be caught in traffic or in a long line. Remember the tension and remember how your body feels that tension. Remember how you react to others in those moments.

Now take a deep breath and let your body relax. Know what it is to feel grace under pressure.

A Call to Conversation

What most tries your patience?

When was a time you lost your patience? What caused it? Who was involved?

What helps you keep your cool when you are under pressure?

Do you see a difference between patience and perseverance? Can you describe it?

When is it hardest and easiest for you to exhibit patience?

What is your reaction to the patience of the "Iron Jawed Angels" and what Martin Luther King Jr. describes?

A Call to Action

The next time you are in a traffic jam, at rush hour or behind a long line at a counter, take a deep breath, smile, and let someone else in ahead of you. Feel a sense of patience in your predicament.

A Call to Prayer

Merciful God, fill our hearts with the fruit of your Holy Spirit: with love, joy, peace, patience, kindness, goodness, gentleness, faithfulness and self-control. Teach us to love those who hate us, pray for those who persecute us and bless those who curse us. Make your sun to shine on the good and the evil; cause your rain to fall on the just and the unjust. In adversity may we be patient; in prosperity, humble. Guard our lips and guide our hands. May we lightly esteem the pleasures of this world and seek after heavenly things; through Jesus Christ our Lord. Amen.

– From St. Anselm

6

KINDNESS

I joke about wanting to become a curmudgeon in my old age, a cantankerous old coot full of spit and vinegar. Not all realize it's a joke. Most people mellow as they age; it probably has as much to do with hormones as it does with wisdom, but I actually do hope that I will mellow. I think I already have, at least some. I haven't beaten any heads against the wall recently, not mine nor some one else's. Maybe part of the mellowing process is just getting tired; things just aren't worth the effort of fighting over them any more.

Hopefully, we gain some perspective with the years. Hopefully, we gain some compassion from our experiences. Hopefully, we gain some humility from being on the bottom as well as on the top. Hopefully, we gain some wisdom and learn from our experiences. Hopefully, we gain some kindness.

Kindness means to be well-fitted or well-suited. It doesn't mean soft and gentle; it simply means it fits well. When I was young and got a new pair of shoes, not hand me downs, genuine new shoes, I had to break them in. New shoes were stiff; if worn too long, they would wear blisters on your feet. You had to wear them around for a while and then take them off and put other shoes on. New shoes were not well-fitted. They might be the right size for your feet, but they were not kind until they were broken in. We may have a favorite chair that is likewise now well fitted for our form.

Courteous might be associated with kindness, as a type of every day kindness. Being well mannered, respectful of others. Saying "please" and "thank you," "yes, ma'am" and "no sir" brings a kindness to our conversation, a genteelness to our relationships. It may be difficult to be kind to the unkind, but a smile and some laughter can work wonders and kindness can be contagious. Kindness also has a sense of tenderness to it, respectful of the feelings and opinions of others. One of our group members shared how he had seen people's attitudes change simply by his asking "Is there something I can do for you?" This offer of kindness toward another and openness to their needs and concerns can defuse a tense situation.

In Matthew, Jesus says, "Come unto me all you who labor and are heavily burdened and I will give you rest. Take my yoke upon you and learn from me, for I am gentle and humble and you will find rest for your souls. My yoke is easy and my burden is light" (Matt 11:28-30). The description of the yoke is interesting. Yes, there is a burden, yes there is a load, but if the yoke is properly balanced, the load will not wear unevenly on those who wear it. With a team of oxen, the yoke can be adjusted so that the stronger ox bears a greater load and the two will be equally yoked. A well fitted yoke means each oxen exerts equal effort, not that each carries the same load. Kindness means the yoke does not chafe.

I have known some who were so kind in their wisdom and wise in their kindness that they could school someone without their knowing or realizing at the time that they were being schooled.

The Greek is sometimes translated "kindness," sometimes "gentleness" (which comes later in our listing), sometimes "sweetness" or "mellowness," like a well-aged wine. "Equanimity," even-tempered, clear minded, composed.

Most wine needs to be aged as part of the wine making process. Fresh wine is stored in large oaken barrels and allowed to age, sometimes for years. Spanish sherry will be stored for twenty five years or longer. The flavor of the wine changes as it ages. It is described as maturing. A skilled wine taster can tell the age of a wine by its taste. I am not encouraging anyone to drink wine. I merely offer this as an example of mellowness, what it means to be kind, even very kind.

Most of us also mature as we age, although I have heard that growing older is mandatory and growing up is optional. We may be energetic and emotional when we are young and become more mellow as we mature.

The Psalms tell us over and over again of God: "great is thy loving kindness," "thy loving kindness is greater than life." This is a kindness that is boldly benevolent.

Perhaps you've seen the bumper sticker that says, "Perform Random Acts of Kindness." The world is filled with too many random acts of violence. We need some kindness, people on the lookout for opportunities to do something good for somebody else for no other reason than the simple pleasure of doing the good. What can I do to brighten somebody's day or lighten somebody's load?

It can be as simple a gesture as letting someone else in line ahead of us, allowing ourselves to be a sounding board for someone else's misery, holding a door for someone who's arms are full. What can I do today to make this corner of the world a little better for my having been here?

Immanuel Kant, the great German philosopher, wrote of the categorical imperative as a universal law which instructs us on how we are to behave:

> Act only, in any circumstance and with any person, as you would have all people act in that instance.

Act in such a way as you would have all people act.

This is a kindness that shows no partiality, a kindness that is truly universal. It is also exactly what Jesus says in the Golden Rule, "Do unto others as you would have them do unto you." Do the right thing because it is the right thing to do, not because we derive any benefit or pleasure from it and not because it will result in something to our advantage. Do right by others simply because it is right.

In the study of philosophy, this principle is called the Rule of Reciprocity. All religions, philosophies and wisdom traditions contain this rule, although usually in a negative sense: "Don't do to others what you don't want done to yourself; don't treat others in a way you don't want to be treated." We can fulfill this rule simply by sitting around and doing nothing. If I don't do anything, I can't do anything I don't want done to me. But it will not satisfy Jesus' version.

Jesus says "Do unto others." He does not say "don't do." As Christians, we cannot fulfill the Golden Rule by sitting around and doing no harm; we have to actively promote the good. "Do unto others!" Christianity is not a spectator sport, there are no innocent bystanders. We are either doing the good or we are in the wrong; there is no "not doing." You've heard the expression from Edmund Burke, "The only thing necessary for evil to triumph in this world is for good people to do nothing." Good people doing nothing doesn't work. We have to do unto others as we would want others to do to us, regardless of how they treat us in return.

We had a woman who was a member of our church and was aptly named Grace. Her daughter was just as well named, Joy. They embodied those expressions of grace and of joy and brought them to others in their daily lives. When shopping, Grace would buy three of everything: one for now, one for later and one for the community food pantry. Grace was indeed kindness in action. Grace had reached her one hundredth birthday and Joy was near eighty, both in a retirement community. Appropriately enough, she died on Valentine's Day, a day of sacrificial love. Her last words were in response to the question asking if she did anything special on Valentine's Day. She replied "Every day is special," and she had lived to make it so. Demonstrating kindness in our daily lives is a way for us to make every day special.

In Micah 6:8 we are reminded, "What does the Lord require of you, but to do justice, to love mercy and to walk humbly with the Lord your God?" Humbly working for justice in a way that demonstrates mercy toward all would certainly reflect this kindness.

Kindness is an attitude of mind and emotion that is mellow and sweet, that is smooth, wise and gentle and that is respectful of the needs and concerns of others. No room to be angry there!

A Call to Reflection

Remember a time when someone else's kindness toward you made a difference to you or in your attitude. What was the situation?

How did you feel in the midst of it?

Who was the other person?

What specific actions did they take to help alleviate your dilemma?

A Call to Conversation

How do you understand kindness and separate it from the other fruits of the Spirit?

How do you connect the prophet's challenge to do justice, love mercy and walk humbly, with the Biblical understanding of kindness?

Do you agree that daily courtesies may be a way of demonstrating kindness?

How have you seen this in your experience?

Immanuel Kant's categorical imperative calls to always do what is right, regardless of the circumstances or outcomes. When has this been difficult in your life?

A Call to Action

What are some "random acts of kindness" you can perform?

How will you perform them?

Where will you be at the time?

Who will be with you?

Plan for random acts of kindness in your day and look for opportunities to perform them.

A Call to Prayer

Give me, O Lord, pure lips, a clean heart and right action. Give me humility and patience, justice and temperance. Give me wisdom and understanding, knowledge and godliness. May I always seek your face in all whom I see and know your presence in all I do. Assist me, God Most High and infinite in mercy, have mercy on me. Amen.

— From the Gallican Sacramentary

7

GOODNESS

J erry Lee Lewis sang "Goodness, gracious, great balls of fire!" While his personal life may not be a good example of it, these words fairly describe what this spiritual fruit of goodness fully is. This is how the dictionary defines it, "satisfactory, virtuous, worthy, benevolent, desirable, favorable, skillful, reliable, considerable, abundant, proven." If I could live up to this half the time, I would be a good man indeed!

The translators mix "kindness" and "goodness" back and forth for two similar Greek words. One difference is that goodness has some backbone to it, some spunk, some "ball of fire." Goodness, says William Barclay, is what Jesus showed when he was clearing the temple. It is a very active, vigorous scene of righteous indignation or holy anger; certainly not a scene of Jesus being meek or mild. Kindness is what Jesus showed when he was with the woman at the well: he initiates the conversation, as a Jewish man to a Samaritan woman breaking several taboos. It is an entirely different scene but no less radical. There is some discipline with goodness, some sense of accountability and consequence.

Kindness might be seen as more relational, whereas goodness might be more behavioral. Kindness relates to our being and who we are; goodness relates to our doing.

Goodness is about doing what is right, not doing what may be popular or favorable. There was a man with a withered hand who approached Jesus on the Sabbath (Matt 12:8-11). Jesus confronted the Pharisees, asking if it was appropriate to do a good, kind, right thing on a day when any form of work was forbidden, and he healed the hand.

As Christians, we call ourselves disciples of Christ. A disciple is more than a follower or well-wisher or hanger-on. A disciple is a student, one who patterns his or her life after that of another, one who uses another as role model. As disciples of Christ, we model our lives after his; he sets the pattern we endeavor to follow. "What would Jesus do" is not just some trite slogan for a bumper sticker or wristband. It is the guiding question of our lives. A disciple has a discipline, a pattern to follow and the way to follow it.

Goodness may be a fruit of the Spirit, but certainly discipline is a gift or a grace of the Spirit and a good thing. Without discipline, goodness would lose its strength. As we exercise our discipline, it becomes easier for us to use our goodness. With discipline, the practice becomes a pattern.

Paul reinforces the idea of the strength and goodness of discipline in 2 Timothy 1:7: "God did not give us a spirit of cowardice, but rather a spirit of power and of love and of self-discipline." When we feel stressed out from worry or exhausted by our schedule, this is a good lesson to remember: we have the spirit of power and love and self-discipline!

Clearly, champions have discipline! Every athlete, every team, practices and drills and prepares for their competition, knowing that if they want to excel, they must first exert themselves, excellence only comes with effort. Why should it be less so with our faith? Can we expect goodness to blossom in our lives without our making an effort for it? Of course not! We know that in every walk of life, success only comes with effort. Exercising our faith in goodness is no different.

Goodness is kind and strong, like kindness with discipline. It is muscular and sinewy and has guts. It is kindness with teeth, "kindness or else!" It is also translated "generosity," so maybe it is kindness with enough to share, kindness in abundance. In 2 Thessalonians 1:11, Paul speaks of God's power working to fulfill our goodness and every act inspired by faith. In Romans 15:14, he connects goodness with knowledge and the ability to encourage, instruct and hold one another accountable. In Ephesians 5:9, he connects it with righteousness and truth. One of our members declared, "Godliness is an element of goodness." Clearly this is a broad and generous term, with backbone and gumption!

Confirmation is a cherished tradition at St. Peter's. Confirmands are to select and memorize a Bible verse and explain why that verse is so important to them. They remember it throughout their lives and often have it read during their funeral services. Phyllis was one such person. Her husband was an entrepreneur and business man and very much the extravert. Phyllis supported him behind the scenes and raised their four girls. She was very much the wind beneath his wings. When she died, she wanted her Confirmation passage read. It was Philippians 4:8, expanding it to include verse 7 reads:

> The peace of God, which passes all understanding, keep your hearts and minds in Christ Jesus. Finally, dear friends, whatever is true, whatever is honorable, whatever is right, whatever is pure, whatever is lovely, whatever is admirable, if there is any excellence, anything worthy of praise, think on these things. Whatever you have learned or received or heard or seen in me, put into practice, and the God of peace will be with you.

Whatever is true, honorable, right, pure, lovely, admirable, excellent, worthy of praise.

This is goodness, this is gracious, and this is a ball of great, cleansing fire.

A Call to Reflection

Make a list of all the things in your life that you would call "good." This might include people and objects, family, friends, hobbies, food. The idea is simply to list everything in your life that is good. Review that list and see how extensive it is, how good your life is. Keep that list where you can find it when you need it, when you need to remember the good that is yours.

A Call to Conversation

How do you define goodness?

How do you distinguish goodness from kindness?

Can you think of examples?

Do you have a favorite Bible verse you have memorized?

How did you select it? How has it helped you?

Have you ever prepared for a competition? How did you prepare for it?

What difference did the practice and preparation make in the outcome?

How does this practice and preparation relate to your Christian discipline?

When was a time that you did the right thing even though it was not popular?

A Call to Action

Keep an eye open today for people doing good things, especially in their daily chores and obligations. Let them know they are appreciated. When someone is good to you, remember to thank them!

A Call to Prayer

O God, to whom glory is sung in the highest and on earth peace, good will, to all; grant that good will to us your children; cleanse us from all wrong and give peace to all your people; through your mercy, O blessed Lord God, who lives in all and reigns over all, world without end. Amen.

8

GENTLENESS

Proverbs 15:1 says "A gentle word turns aside anger, but harsh words stir up wrath." We have all seen the truth of both sides of this verse. If I am trying to curb my anger, learning some gentleness would be a good idea. Jesus describes himself as gentle in Matthew 11:28-30: "Come to me, all you that are weary and heavily burdened, and I will give you rest. Take my yoke upon you and learn from me, for I am gentle and humble in heart, and you will find rest for your souls. My yoke is easy and my burden is light." The attitude of gentleness also seems to be described in the 23rd Psalm. Maybe the reason there are so many popular scriptural descriptions of gentleness is because we could all use some.

But we don't have to go to the Bible to find instances of gentleness. In the mid 1960's there was a Saturday morning cartoon show featuring Milton the Monster who was like a humorous Frankenstein. He had been assembled from various spare parts by Professor Weirdo and Count Kook. He was big and strong. During his creation, Dr. Professor Weirdo and Count Kook used six drops of the essence of terror and five drops of sinister sauce, but also a tincture of tenderness, lest he destroy those who created him. Of course, they used too much tenderness and ended up with a very gentle and kind monster. Maybe that's the kind of curmudgeon I'll be.

As Otis Redding sang in his rhythm and blues hit, *Try a Little Tenderness*, we all need to try a little tenderness and to speak soft words gently. Tenderness, gentleness, consideration. In the Beatitudes, the same word is translated meek: "Blessed are the meek, for they will inherit the earth" (Matthew 5:5).

I used to think that being meek was a bad thing, like being walked on or taken advantage of. Learning of Aristotle's Golden Mean, I found a different definition. Aristotle thought of this meekness as being perfectly angry: angry at the right time, in the right way, with the right expression, toward the right end, with the right focus, to the right measure, etc. Meekness as righteous anger? I've encountered people who felt that righteous anger, and I would not call them meek!

The Greek word translated as gentleness might also be translated as meekness, tenderness, modesty, courtesy or considerateness. A very respectful person, like Bob Cratchit from Charles Dickens' *A Christmas Carol* might come to mind, but there is more to it than that. Aristotle's Golden mean considers virtues to be the perfect balance between the excesses of either too much or too little. Courage is the virtuous balance between the excesses of too much, foolhardiness, and too little, cowardice. Moderation in food is the virtuous balance between too much, gluttony, and too little, starvation. Generosity is the virtuous balance between being wasteful and being stingy. Meekness is the perfect, virtuous balance between the extremes of being a hot-head and being a doormat.

This is clearly not a passive virtue. Jesus gives us an example of this meek gentleness when the Pharisees confront him with a woman caught in adultery: "Let the one without sin cast the first stone." And "Neither do I condemn you, go and sin no more" (John 8:3-11). Again, in clearing the money changers and merchants from the temple, Jesus shows us a more vigorous example of what Aristotle meant by meekness, being angry at the right time, for the right cause, with the right expression, in the right manner. Quoting from Isaiah, he says, "My house shall be a house of prayer for all people, and you have made it a den of thieves" (Mark 11:16-18)!

The word that in Galatians is translated "gentleness" is also the word that in the Beatitudes is translated "meek." "Blessed are the meek, for they shall inherit the earth" (Matt 5:11). The meek walk gently upon the earth, mindful of the impact their presence has on others who live here, realizing that creation is a "community of subjects, not a collection of objects," as Thomas Berry says.

"Gentle" is the word we add to man to describe a gentleman, a man who is polite, courteous, respectful, etc. Originally, "gentleman" simply meant a man who was nobly born. A man could be a louse, rogue and scoundrel, but if his father was a lord, he would still be a gentleman. This is not what we mean today! We expect a gentleman to be gentle.

There was an old Chrysler car commercial filled with images of families enjoying their Chrysler cars. One scene was a huge towering man with broad muscular shoulders, viewed from the back. In his arms he held a tiny, fragile baby. This is the image that comes to my mind with "gentle." One who has the power, has the strength, and chooses not to use it, who practices restraint. Practicing restraint is part of being gentle. Only the strong can be gentle.

Another television show from the '70's was "Gentle Ben," the story of a big bear who, despite his great strength, could also be quite gentle. Maybe strength is a pre-condition for gentleness. Maybe it takes a person confident in his or her own strength to be able to show gentleness.

One of the books on my shelf is titled *Ride the Wild Horses*, a collection of sermons. In the title sermon, the author speaks of our urges and impulses and the energy they provide. He uses the analogy of wild horses and argues that we do not want to break their spirit or tame them, but we do want to be able to bridle them and to ride them, to use the energy of these impulses in ways that are positive and constructive. Again, being gentle requires restraint.

At the end of *Magnum Force*, Clint Eastwood as Dirty Harry shares one of his several memorable quotes, "A man's got to know his limitations." Part of gentleness is knowing one's limitations, being teachable and willing to submit to that teaching. I don't do all things well, but Becki says in my defense, "He's educable." Modesty and humility are a part of gentleness.

In what seems to be a lifetime ago, Henri Nouwen wrote a series of articles for *Sojourners* on downward mobility as part of the

Christian vocation (June, July and August 1981). I was so moved by those articles I saved them; I have copies of them and still review them from time to time. I have several of his books, but these three articles seem to distill Nouwen's teaching: *The Selfless Way of Christ: Downward Mobility as Christian Vocation, Temptation: The Pull Toward Upward Mobility*, and *A Self-Emptied Heart: The Disciplines of Spiritual Formation*. In these articles, he is inspired by Philippians 2:5-11 and the *kenosis* or self-emptying of God in Christ. This passage is a perfect example of the downward way of Christ and a call to a life of gentleness. God is a gentle God!

We've all known people who have been described in these few pages. For me, one was my high school math teacher, Mr. Fred Smith. Fred had a small farm outside of town which he loved to work and he had the build to prove it, looking more like a farmer than a teacher. In my senior year he taught calculus and trigonometry, teaching us how to calculate the odds of something by learning how to shoot craps and calculating our chances with the dice. In college I took a math class in logic that I just could not get; it seemed totally foreign. Desperate, when I was home visiting, I called Fred and begged him to help. He protested that it would be beyond his ability but I insisted. He took the book overnight and studied it and the next day in two hours explained what I could not fathom from nearly a full term. In simple common terms, and with calm patience, he explained it to me in a way I could understand. For me, his was an example of gentleness as true as anything in scripture.

I can be Milton and use a tincture of tenderness to temper my monstrous temper. I can heed Otis Redding and try a little tenderness or be a bear known as Gentle Ben. I can follow Dirty Harry and know my limitations. I can learn to ride the wild horses without breaking or taming them. I can listen to Aristotle and practice that dynamic balance between being a hot-head and a doormat. I can be that anonymous gentle giant, carefully cradling the infant in his massive strong arms. Maybe I can even live up to the example of my math teacher Fred Smith. I can learn to be a true gentleman!

A Call to Reflection

Recall a time in your life when a gentle act was also an act that required strength or restraint. Maybe being picked up as a child or held as an infant. Consider how strength and gentleness relate.

A Call to Conversation

When was a time you had to practice restraint, to exercise your will to refrain from doing something that you had the power to do, but knew you ought not do it?

Who have been your favorite teachers? What characteristics made them to be so?

When was a time someone else was gentle with you?

What is your reaction to connecting a spirit of gentleness with a sense of holy anger? What is your response to Jesus' clearing the temple? What emotions do you think he was feeling?

A Call to Action

Find the opportunity to hold a baby in your arms. Let yourself fully experience that moment. Feel both the gentleness and the strength, the trust and the restraint. Know what it is to be held so gently and so strongly by a gracious, loving, powerful God.

A Call to Prayer

O Lord, we ask in your mercy to receive our prayers and grant us the wisdom to know what we ought to do and ought not do, and grace and strength to so fulfill your teaching; through Christ our Lord. Amen.
— Gregorian Sacramentary

9

FAITHFULNESS

F aith is belief or trust. It describes our relationship with, our response to and our reliance upon the absolute otherness of God. Hebrews 11:1 says, "Faith is the assurance of things hoped for, the conviction of things not seen." Faithfulness carries with it a sense of loyalty or steadfastness.

A verse I often repeat is Psalm 115:1, "Not to us, O Lord, not ever to us, but to thy name be glory, to thy name be praise, for thy abiding love toward us and thy steadfast faithfulness." As the hymn repeats,

> Great is Thy faithfulness!
> Morning by morning new mercies I see;
> all I have needed thy hand hath provided.
> Great is thy faithfulness, Lord unto me!"

I can never match God's faithfulness, yet that is what we are called to model, to incarnate in our lives. We are called Christian, after Jesus, who is the "faithful and true witness" of Revelation 3:14. Our challenge is to be as faithful in following Christ as Christ was in following the will of God as he understood it.

At the beginning his ministry, Jesus spent forty days in the wilderness in fasting and prayer, tempted to live out his witness in different ways. In turning stone to bread, he was tempted to lead a ministry of comfort and ease, of physical gratification in the here and now, much like the "prosperity gospel" that is so much a part of contemporary televised evangelists. In the challenge to throw himself down from the temple mount, he was tempted to the spectacular and grandiose, to satisfying his own ego rather than humbling himself in the example of servant leadership; as Mother Theresa said, "doing small tasks with great love." In the temptation to serve Satan, Jesus faced the dilemma we all do in offering our full service to anything that is not of God, giving ultimate allegiance to that which is not ultimate. Faithfulness is what Jesus showed in standing firm and staying true to his calling, to that which fed the core of his being and expressed the fullest of the divine will in his life.

Faithfulness is what Jesus showed in the garden before his arrest. "If it be possible, let this cup pass," he asked. He expressed his will, his desire, even gave voice to his fear, but that was not the end of it: "Nevertheless, not my will but thine be done." "I have given my word and I will be true; if need be, I will shake hands with that cross." Christ is the faithful and true witness, who gave his word even in his death and who therefore triumphed over the grave.

Faithfulness is what Eugene Peterson describes in his book, *A Long Obedience in a Constant Direction: Discipleship in an Instant Society.* Faithfulness is what Winston Churchill describes, "never, never, never, never, never give up!" or Muhammad Ali, "What counts is not how many times you get knocked down, but how many times you get back up."

There is a determination to this faithfulness, a perseverance. This faithfulness is like the bulldog of our faith: taking hold, clenching tight, and holding on, like the Eveready or Die Hard battery or the pink Energizer bunny or the Timex watch that "takes a licking and keeps on ticking."

Faithful means being constant in one's relationships, but it does not mean unchanging. We all change. If I am to remain constant in my relationship with you, then I must adjust and adapt as you change and you must adjust and adapt as I change. Indeed, constancy in our relationships may require us to change!

"Martyr" describes someone who died for their faith, their beliefs. It is from the Greek word *martyrion*, meaning "witness." It has the connotation that it does today because of the faithful witnessing of the early church. Christians stayed true to their beliefs under persecution, torture and execution. They demonstrated and declared their faith even though it meant sacrificing their lives; they stayed true to death. Their witness had such a strong impact on the pagan Roman society that the word for witness became the word for one who died for what they believed, one who remained faithful to the end.

Gail and David were a beautiful young couple who had met in college and got married. David graduated early and joined the Navy; Gail went back to campus to finish her degree. Some months later Gail was home visiting and came to church.

"How's it going?" I asked innocently after worship.

Gail looked at me with a kind of frozen shock. "We thought we knew what love is." She stated with unexpected intensity. "We didn't." She paused, focusing her thoughts. "Love isn't some kind of warm feeling. It isn't romance and flowers." It was like she was discovering this as she spoke. "Love is commitment."

I had another couple that wanted to change their vows from "as long as we both shall live" to "as long as love shall last." I talked them out of it, with the same realization that had come to Gail. Feelings come and go, emotions wax and wane; you can't build a relationship on them. For love to last, it needs a more solid foundation. Love that is lasting, love that will see you through the storms, requires commitment.

Love is commitment. Love is giving your word and sticking with it, no matter what. As C.S. Lewis says in *Mere Christianity*, "Christian love, either towards God or towards one another, is an affair of the will."

This kind of faithfulness, this deep and abiding loyalty, bears the fruit of confidence, which literally means "with faithfulness." In my first church after seminary, we had a large active youth group that pushed one another to be confident Christians. We made long sleeved tee shirts that had the word "Confidence" spelled down one sleeve. On the front, it said, "I'm a confident Christian – bring on the lions!" and a picture of a chubby little Christian with a big smile and a tall cross, standing over a knocked out lion. I still have that shirt and pray that I may yet have that confidence.

It may be that confident faithfulness is like any other habit: the more you exercise it, the easier it gets. Any action we practice regularly becomes a habit; some say after twenty-one days, some say after twenty-eight days. Our thoughts become our words, become our acts, become our habits, become our character. I want the character of a confident, faithful Christian!

Faithfulness means giving your word and sticking to it: true, loyal, reliable, trustworthy, unwavering, fidelity, constancy. There was a time when contracts were sealed with a simple handshake, when your word was your bond. Psalm 15 asks the question, "O Lord, who may abide in your tent? Who may dwell on your holy hill" (v. 1)? Part of the response is "Those who stand by their oath even to their hurt" (v.4).

Steadfast faithfulness is what Shel Silverstein describes in his book *The Giving Tree*, a fable about a tree that loves a boy and gives itself entirely to the boy: its leaves, its fruit, its branches, its trunk and finally its stump. The tree gave itself in love entirely to the boy, and in the giving the tree found happiness. The risk in faithfulness is that the trusting, the giving, must come before there is proof or evidence of the reliability of the recipient. We must be vulnerable and open ourselves up to the other, trusting that they will respond in kind and knowing that sometimes they won't. Faithfulness means that we must be willing to be hurt sometimes.

Faithfulness is what Spock portrayed in *Star Trek Two: The Wrath of Khan*. The ship is in danger and the battle seems lost. Spock goes to the engine room and enters a radiation chamber to restore power, at the sacrifice of his life. Captain Kirk rushes in with an attempt to save him, but it is too late. Spock's last words to his captain were "I am, and have always been, your friend." A friend who serves, even at great personal sacrifice.

Faithfulness means to stand "at the ready." Dennis Rodman played basketball for the Chicago Bulls as part of their team that won three consecutive championships. With a nickname of "The

Worm" and covered with tattoos, he had a reputation as something of a wild man, both in the league and in public, but he was a fierce competitor and leading rebounder. He knew his role. I remember watching games on TV and there would be Dennis, peddling hard on an exercise bike to keep his muscles loose and warm, ready to go in, on the side lines, but always ready to give his best, his all. However crazy he might have been, he was faithful. He knew his role and he was always ready to fill it.

My son Joshua joined the Marines when he realized he wasn't ready for college. Their motto is *Semper Fi*, always prepared, always ready, always faithful. He joined before 9/11, and that changed his assignments. He was in the Persian Gulf twice before the invasion and in Iraq afterward. After their second tour to the Gulf, I went to visit while they were at Miramar Air Base in San Diego. I sat in the Ready Room with them at the end of their shift. They shared their experiences and expectations from their recent deployment. They had three things to say: "It is an indefensible position, we have no business being there, and we know we're going back." *Semper Fi*! Always faithful, always prepared.

Hans Christian Andersen has a fairy tale about the little tin soldier who falls in love with a paper ballerina. He gives her his all, his best. He stands at attention, admiring and honoring her. In the end, he is melted down in an oven in the form of a heart. The heart of love is commitment for another that is constant. Like the tin soldier, like the giving tree, like Jesus Christ, in our faithfulness we give ourselves fully and freely to the other, the beloved.

A Call to Reflection

Consider all the people in your life whom you have loved or been loved by. Consider all the occasions when you have felt loved. Now consider how faithfulness is a part of that love, how commitment offers a foundation upon which that love can grow and flourish.

A Call to Conversation

When have you given your word and found it difficult to keep, or wish you hadn't?

When have you been disappointed by someone else who did not keep their word?

What is your reaction to the thought of love as commitment?

How do you understand the difference between constancy and unchanging? How have you adjusted to changes in order to remain constant in a relationship?

A Call to Action

Who has been your best and truest friend, the one who is available when needed and willing to help when called upon? Spend some time with them, whether in person, by phone or computer. Let them know you value that friendship.

A Call to Prayer

O God, the light of every heart that sees you, the life of every soul that loves you, the strength of every mind that seeks you, grant me to continue steadfast in your love. Be the joy of my heart: take it and dwell there. It is too narrow; expand and enlarge it. It lies in ruins; repair and restore it. It is filled with filth; cleanse and claim it. Cleanse me from secret faults and presumptuous sins. May you always have dominion in my life. Amen.

— From St. Augustine

10

SELF-CONTROL

If you've never thought of self-control as being a fruit and work of the Holy Spirit, you've never seen someone really angry. We have covered eight fruits of the Holy Spirit, eight good and godly reasons for not losing one's anger: love, joy, peace, patience, kindness, goodness, gentleness, and faithfulness. That should be reason enough. But if not, there is always the punch line of self-control.

I could count to ten and still be angry — use it as an occasion to build up steam. There are only nine fruit, not ten, but that does not mean there is one lacking. It is awkward, embarrassing and shameful, as well as inconsistent, to get to the end of that list, land on "self-control," and then be angry.

The body is intended to be the servant of the will, the flesh of the spirit. Paul writes about this struggle. "The good that I would do, I do not. The wrong I would avoid, I do" (Rom 7:19)! He shares his frustrations with this inner warfare, "Wretched man that I am! Who will save me from this body of death" (Romans 7:24)?

Paul writes about the discipline required for self-control: "Do you not know that in a race the runners all compete, but only one received the prize? Run in such a way that you may win it. Athletes exercise self-control in all things; they do it to receive a perishable wreath, but we an imperishable one. So I do not run aimlessly, nor do I box as though beating the air; but I punish my body and enslave it, so that after proclaiming to others I myself should not be disqualified" (1 Cor 9:24-27).

In high school cross country, our races were two miles long. Our practice runs were three to five miles, or we would run "speed laps" around the track, sprinting the straightways and jogging the curves. Our practices were always longer and tougher than our competitions.

In my junior year, we had a lot of fun running cross country but we didn't win many meets; our record was 3-22. Our coach was also our varsity basketball coach, and cross country was just a filler for him. As long as we didn't cause any trouble, we could do what we wanted. We had fun, but we didn't win much.

My senior year we got a different coach. Coach Roy Sneed was a former Marine, and true to form, there was nothing "former" about him. Everything he did was at his best. I think he pushed himself to drive to school at his very best. He pushed us hard; I remember vomiting after many of our practices, which were like miniature boot camp experiences. He gave us a pattern to follow, a practice to bring out excellence. It was work, not fun; we were disciplined. He made us better than we thought we could be. We finished 23-2 and county champions. If you want to win, if you want to be a champion, you've got to have discipline!

James repeats the importance of self-control in his chapter on the tongue. "We put bits into the mouths of horses and control their whole body. Large ships are guided by small rudders. So with the tongue: it is a small member but a mighty force" (James 3:3-5).

We have all said things we have come to regret. In this age of instant messaging with text and email, words written in haste or anger may come back to haunt us. As Edward Fitzgerald writes in his translation of the *Rubaiyat of Omar Khayyam*: "The moving finger writes and having writ, moves on: nor all your piety nor wit shall lure it back to cancel half a line, nor all your tears wash out a word of it." I've used a prayer to help me with this, "May my words this day be soft and gentle, for tomorrow I may have to eat them."

The childhood verse, "Sticks and stones may break my bones, but words will never hurt them" proves to be false. Instead of bruising the body, they bruise the soul; instead of wounding the flesh, they wound the spirit. And those inner wounds and hidden bruises are much harder to heal.

There is a story of an Indian boy preparing for his initiation to become a warrior. He is taken aside by his grandfather, a wise and experienced warrior, who describes a terrible fight being waged within the boy between two wolves. One wolf is anger, hate, fear, dread. The other wolf is confidence, hope, trust, wisdom. "Which wolf will win?" asks the boy. The grandfather replies, "The one you feed." The greatest struggle any of us have is over our own will. If we can win that inner war, we can face any outer struggle with confidence.

The book of Revelation speaks of a great cosmic conflict. Every move we make, every word we say, every deed we do, makes a difference in that struggle. How we choose affects the outcome; how we decide makes a difference.

I've heard that the line between heaven and hell is drawn through each human heart. We determine the balance. Cultures and traditions around the world and throughout history have declared that the greatest conquest, the greatest mastery one can claim is the mastery of one's will, the conquest of one's emotions. Before we can master the world we must first master ourselves.

Self-control is the mastery of one's will and emotions. It is the athlete's disciplined mastery of his or her body. In government, self-control means there is no private influence in public policy. Self-control is not apathy, nor the Stoic's passive resignation. This self-control is vigilant, active, dynamic, always on watch.

I heard the story of a man who always greeted people when walking along the street. He would greet each person cheerily, with a smile on his face and a lift in his voice. Some responded in kind, some muttered or mumbling a kind of non-greeting, others simply ignored him. When asked why he stayed so positive when he received negative responses, he asked, "Why should I let their attitude determine mine?" It is easy for us to be reactors rather than actors, to let other people set our agenda or determine our attitude. Yet there is a freedom to be found in exercising our self-control. We determine our behavior independent of how other people choose to act. With self-control we can be actors rather than re-actors.

Self-control finds its contentment in wanting what we have rather than having all we might want. Sometimes translated "temperance," it is more than that. It is "restraint," as in the leash restraining the dog during a walk or the bridle restraining the horse from running wild. Restraining is retraining. In the painting *The Peaceable Kingdom* all the wild animals of the forest are depicted together, the lion with the lamb and the wolf with the kid. This peace is maintained by the vigilant self-control of the meat-eaters, as you can tell by their tightly clenched jaws. Self-control is active, not passive.

Edward Hicks was a Quaker minister who made his living as a painter. Born in 1780 and dying in 1849, his father was a Loyalist who lost everything after the Revolution; his mother died when he was eighteen months old. He started by painting signs and orna-mentation. Starting in 1826, he painted over sixty versions of *The Peaceable Kingdom*, based on Isaiah 11:6-9:

> The wolf shall live with the lamb,
>> the leopard shall lie down with the kid,
>> the calf and the lion and the fatling together,
>> and a little child shall lead them.
> The cow and the bear shall graze,
>> their young shall lie down together;
>> and the lion shall eat straw like the ox.
> The nursing child shall play
>> over the hole of the asp,
>> and the weaned child shall put its hand
>> on the adder's den.
> They will not hurt or destroy
>> on all my holy mountain;
>> for the earth will be full
>> of the knowledge of the Lord
>> as the waters cover the sea.

The image of bears grazing and lions eating straw indicates how important it is that the strong exert self-control if we are to live together in peace and harmony. Converting carnivores to herbivores is a mighty transformation indeed! If these instinctual drives can be controlled, then surely so can my anger.

I admit to my anger, which needs to be controlled. Yet there is energy in that anger, power to be used. If it can be controlled, if it can be managed, and directed, then the energy can be used for good. The wild horses don't need to be tamed or broken; they do need to be bridled, so that their energy can be focused and directed. Paul writes "Be angry, but without sin" (Eph 4:26). It is possible to use the energy of anger in ways that can be positive and constructive rather than negative and destructive; we need to focus that energy.

With self-control riding over the other fruits of the spirit, managing and directing them as a conductor directs an orchestra, even I can manage, control, direct my anger. Self-control calls out the other fruit as they are necessary and appropriate: how much to love, where to highlight joy, when to call for peace, strength to remain patient, courage to be kind, thoughtful enough to be good, vulnerable enough to be gentle, endurance to be faithful. Self-control is the mastery of the self and the management of the fruit that make for a fruitful, fulfilling life.

A Call to Reflection

Remember a time you lost your self-control. What led up to it? How did it happen?

How did you recover? What were the circumstances? What were the consequences?

What did you learn from the experience?

A Call to Conversation

Where is your self-control most tested? What helps you stand firm?

How is self-control the lynch pin or capstone that holds the other virtues together?

What endeavors in your life have you had to exert self-discipline in order to attain success?

A Call to Action

See how long you can hold your breath. Use a stop watch and make three attempts. Breathing is a natural, automatic and necessary part of our existence. Our self-control can suspend it but not prevent it. In our spiritual life, what is equally natural, automatic and necessary? How can the fruit of the Spirit build on it?

A Call to Prayer

Lord God Almighty, you rule over all you have created. We pray that you would guide us better than we can guide ourselves: toward you and your will, and our own deepest need. Strengthen us within and shield us without, that we may ever stand before you in purity. You are our maker and redeemer, our creator and comfort; all praise and glory be to you, now and forever. Amen.

— From Alfred the Great

11

TRANSFORMATION: SO WHAT?

We all start out as little babies. Babies are only capable of doing four things, three of which are not very pretty; they can eat, cry and mess, none of which is very appealing, and they can sleep. Most babies are cute when asleep. Babies are filled with their own needs; they see the world as an extension of themselves. "Mommy and Daddy exist to get me what I want!" And babies want what they want when they want it.

As we grow from babies to toddlers, we learn that other people are not simply extensions of ourselves. We learn we are expected to share with them, that these other people have their own wants. We begin learning how to balance what others want with what we want so that all get something; call it balance or harmony or cooperation.

Toddlers grow into children, children into youth, youth into adults. At each stage, we grow in our understanding of other and the balance between conflicting wants changes. As adults, our focus transfers from ourselves and our wants to our children and their needs. As we grow, hopefully we mature. Growing older is mandatory, growing up is optional!

In his great Love chapter, Paul writes, "When I was a child, I spoke like a child, I thought as a child, I reasoned as a child; when I became an adult, I put away my childish things" (1 Cor 12:11). A baby throwing a fit is normal. A toddler having a tantrum happens regularly. Children will have their fights and need to learn how to work things out. Adults are not supposed to be given to bouts of anger and rage. Behavior that is cute at 4 is embarrassing at 40. At 4 it is child-like; at 40 it is childish.

Paul reminds us that this maturing, this growing up, is a matter of will. We have to want to change and actively choose it. "I appeal to you, brothers and sisters, by the mercies of God, to present your bodies as a living sacrifice, holy and acceptable to God, which is your spiritual worship. Do not be conformed to this world, but be transformed by the renewing of your minds, so that you may discern what is the will of God: what is good and acceptable and perfect" (Rom 12:1-2).

We can mature, we can grow up, but we have to want to!

When my son Jason was young, he would get angry and throw fits. We lived in a mobile home that had shag carpet and he could bang his head on that floor without hurting himself. The carpet offered padding and the floor offered give. We were at the mall one time and Jason had a fit. The mall had cement floors. He banged his head one time on that floor and never had another tantrum or threw another fit.

When I was in high school we had open lunches for an hour and fifteen minutes in the middle of the day. That is a long time for adolescents to wander the streets of the community and look for something to do. We would get bored. Nearly every noon, there was a fight breaking out somewhere, out of sheer boredom. The school adjusted the day so that we only had forty five minutes for lunch, enough time to eat, not enough time to get bored or to fight.

When we are children, we throw temper tantrums. When we are children, we complain of being bored. As Paul writes in 1 Corinthians 13, when we become adults, we put away childish things.

If we don't learn from our mistakes we are bound to repeat them. If we learn from them, at least we can keep life interesting by making different mistakes the next time. Having information does not necessarily make us better people or more complete human beings. If we can process the information, digest it and let it work on us, we have the possibility of growing from the experience. We can transform.

After Paul lists these nine fruit of the Spirit, he then concludes, "against these, there is no law." We like the sound of freedom, the idea of liberty, the concept of independence. We like living a boundless life, a life that is truly free. True freedom means the rules no longer apply, like Neo in the final scene of *The Matrix*. He makes his own rules, creates his own game, shapes his own destiny. He found himself and focused his energy. When he had done this, he became that "against which there is no law" (Gal 5:23).

Earlier in Galatians, Paul writes, "For freedom Christ has set us free. Stand firm, then, and do not submit again to a yoke of slavery" (Gal 5:1). Jesus says, "If you continue in my word, you are my disciples. You will know the truth, and the truth will set you free" (John 8:31-32). When we bear the fruit of the Spirit, we live a life that is free, "against which there is no law."

The way to accomplish this is not by focusing on the fruit, but by focusing on Christ. Jesus says, "I am the vine, you are the branches. Those who abide in me and I in them bear much fruit" (John 15:5). We bear fruit as we abide in Christ. As we abide in Christ, our lives become more and more fruitful and fulfilling. As Paul writes, "The secret of the ages, the mystery of life, has been revealed to us, which is Christ in you, the hope of glory" (Col 1:26-7).

Thomas Merton has a wonderfully simple illustration of this: "How does an apple ripen? It just sits in the sun." Not by tightening its muscles, squinting its eyes or squaring its jaw, but simply by abiding: staying connected to the tree and absorbing the warmth of the sun the fruit matures.

When we live a life that is shaped by and filled with these fruit, then we are fully free. We live a life that is abundant and fruitful and free. The fruitful life is not based on outer circumstance but rather inner certainties, not passing fads but an abiding faith. If we abide in Christ and Christ in us, then we will bear much fruit, fruit that endures. We will enjoy lives that are fruitful, abundant, and fulfilled.

I admit that my temper still lives within me. It is there; I can feel it inside me. I admit that from time to time it still slips free of its bridle. Most of the time it is in check. It has strength that I want to use; it has energy I want to harness. I can ride this wild horse.

I have also learned to cultivate the fruit of the Spirit. I have a life that is far better than any thing I deserve. I am surrounded by love, filled with joy, know a peace that is unshakeable, exercise patience under duress, exercise kindness toward others and find goodness even in adversaries, am trying to be gentle even with myself and model God's own steadfast faithfulness in my relationships with others. I am far from perfect, not near complete. As Paul writes in the verses that could serve as my tombstone:

> Not that I have already been made complete, but I press on to lay hold of that for which Christ Jesus laid hold of me. I do not regard myself as having laid hold of it already, but this one thing I do: forgetting what lies behind and reaching forward to what lies ahead, I press on toward the goal for the prize of the upward call of God that is ours in Jesus Christ our Lord. (Philippians 3:12-14)

I am far from perfect and always have reason to repent, but I am not finished yet. As in the Gaither's song, *I'm Not What I Want to Be*: "I'm not what I want to be, I'm not what I'm going to be, but thank God, I'm not what I was."

The fruitful life is real and obtainable, and worth the effort!

A Call to Reflection

Remember how you felt when you began this study. What were your expectations?

What questions or reluctance did you have?

How has this study met your expectations?

How has it fallen short?

How has it helped?

What have you learned?

A Call to Conversation

Share the experiences you have had as a result of this study. What surprises did you encounter?

What obstacles have you overcome? Particularly, how has *A Call to Action* impacted your study and your life?

A Call to Action

By this time, you probably have Galatians 5:22-23 memorized, "The fruit of the Spirit are these: love, joy, peace, patience, kindness, goodness, gentleness, faithfulness, self-control; against these, there is no law." Use that as a breath prayer, repeating it over and again throughout the day. See if remembering these words has an affect on your attitude and action, your bearing and behavior. See if others notice a difference.

A Call to Prayer

Teach us, good Lord, to serve you as you deserve: to give and not to count the cost; to fight and not to heed the wounds; to toil and not to seek for rest; to labor and not to ask for any reward, save that of knowing we do your will; through Jesus Christ our Lord. Amen.

– Ignatius of Loyola

APPENDIX

Christopher Grundy is a contemporary Christian music artist who composes most of his own songs. You can check him out at: www.christophergrundy.com. One of his compositions is entitled *Fruits of the Spirit*. It is a great, fun, inspiring song! He makes a fruit salad of the fruit of the Spirit!

1.   **Fruits of the Spirit**

The pineapple of patience,
the lime of love,
the kiwi of kindness,
For the kind of world you're dreaming of!

The grapefruit of gentleness,
the peach of peace,
the fig of forgiveness,
Spirit grant me these!

The star fruit of self-control,
the guava of generosity,
Fuji apple of faithfulness,
The jackfruit of joy, Oh Spirit, please!

BIBLIOGRAPHY

Barclay, William. *The Letters to the Galatians and Ephesians*. The Daily Study Bible. Westminster Press, Philadelphia. 1958.

Duncan, George. *The Epistle of Paul to the Galatians*. Harper and Brothers, New York. 1934.

Dunnam, Maxie. *Alive in Christ: The Dynamic Process of Spiritual Formation*. Abingdon, Nashville. 1982.

Foster, Richard J. *Celebration of Discipline: The Path to Spiritual Growth*. Harper and Row, New York. 1978.

Hamilton, J. Wallace. *Ride the Wild Horses: The Christian Use of our Untamed Impulses*. Abingdon, Nashville. 1980.

Hunter, A.M. *Galatians, Ephesians, Philippians, Colossians*. The Layman's Bible Commentaries. SCM Press, London. 1959.

Juliana of Norwich. *Revelations of Divine Love*. Translated by M.L. del Mastro. Image Books, Garden City, New York. 1977.

Lewis, C.S. *The Four Loves*. Harcourt, Brace, Jovanovich, New York. 1960.

_____. *Mere Christianity*. Fontana Books, London. 1960.

_____. *Surprised by Joy*. Harcourt, Brace Jovanovich, New York. 1955.

Neill, Stephen. *Paul to the Galatians*. Association Press, New York. 1958.

Neil, William. *The Letter of Paul to the Galatians*. The Cambridge Bible Commentary. Cambridge University Press, Cambridge, England. 1967.

Peterson, Eugene. *A Long Obedience in the Same Direction: Discipleship in an Instant Society.* Inter Varsity Press Books, Downers Grove, IL. 2000.

Potts, J. Manning, ed. *Prayers of the Early Church*. The Upper Room, Nashville. 1953

Prayers of the Middle Ages. The Upper Room, Nashville. 1954

Silverstein, Shel. *The Giving Tree*. Harper and Row, New York. 1954.

Stagg, Frank. *Galatians and Romans*. Knox Preaching Guides. John Knox Press, Atlanta. 1980.

Stamm, Raymond and Oscar Fisher Blackwelder. *The Epistle to the Galatians*. The Interpreter's Bible. Abingdon Press, Nashville. 1953.

Van de Weyer, Robert. *On Living Simply: The Golden Voice of John Chrysostom*. Liguori/Triumph, Liguori, Missouri. 1997.

Wink, Walter. *Jesus and Nonviolence: A Third Way*. Fortress Press, Minneapolis. 2003.

God created the world we live in. In fact, God created the universe.

So what?

This should be required reading for all clergy early in their careers.

Susan Nienaber
Senior Consultant
The Alban Institute

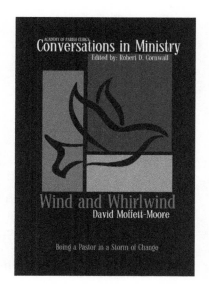

MORE FROM ENERGION PUBLICATIONS

Personal Study

Finding My Way in Christianity	Herold Weiss	$16.99
Holy Smoke! Unholy Fire	Bob McKibben	$14.99
The Jesus Paradigm	David Alan Black	$17.99
When People Speak for God	Henry Neufeld	$17.99
The Sacred Journey	Chris Surber	$11.99

Christian Living

Faith in the Public Square	Robert D. Cornwall	$16.99
Grief: Finding the Candle of Light	Jody Neufeld	$8.99
My Life Story	Becky Lynn Black	$14.99
Crossing the Street	Robert LaRochelle	$16.99
Life as Pilgrimage	David Moffett-Moore	14.99

Bible Study

Learning and Living Scripture	Lentz/Neufeld	$12.99
From Inspiration to Understanding	Edward W. H. Vick	$24.99
Philippians: A Participatory Study Guide	Bruce Epperly	$9.99
Ephesians: A Participatory Study Guide	Robert D. Cornwall	$9.99

Theology

Creation in Scripture	Herold Weiss	$12.99
Creation: the Christian Doctrine	Edward W. H. Vick	$12.99
The Politics of Witness	Allan R. Bevere	$9.99
Ultimate Allegiance	Robert D. Cornwall	$9.99
History and Christian Faith	Edward W. H. Vick	$9.99
The Journey to the Undiscovered Country	William Powell Tuck	$9.99
Process Theology	Bruce G. Epperly	$4.99

Ministry

Clergy Table Talk	Kent Ira Groff	$9.99
Out of This World	Darren McClellan	$24.99

Generous Quantity Discounts Available
Dealer Inquiries Welcome
Energion Publications — P.O. Box 841
Gonzalez, FL_ 32560
Website: http://energionpubs.com
Phone: (850) 525-3916